HUMAN RESOURCES DEVELOPMENT (HRD)

FOR

THE CHIEF EXECUTIVE OFFICER (CEO)

AUTHOR

DR. SIBRAM NISONKO, M.A., PH.D.

MARCH 2021

PREFACE

For various reasons business and industry have great

powers to bring about changes in the society. These

changes have necessarily to start from within. As the economy grows industries also grow. Many times it has to reflect on the role it has been playing and the role that is expected with change of time and understanding.

In this context I have felt that the Chief Executive Officers (CEO) of small companies, the Head of Non-Government organizations and chiefs of autonomous bodies and cooperative entities have to undergo a great change. We can't expect any change in society or business without their change and their support.

In this book I have tried to share my experiences and the experiences of great thinkers on the emerging social crises and the revised role the CEOs have to play to solve such problems.

I have defined who is an achieving CEO. In this book I have presented my thoughts step by step covering the process of HRD for a CEO with an analysis of his role in building the organizational culture, management of change, quality of work life, his primary duties, responsibilities, core values and attitudes and finally his responsibilities as an integrator.

I hope anybody who has interest in industries will find the book useful to ignite his thoughts. I shall be happy if the students of Business Management find it worth reading and reflecting. I shall be looking forward to the response of the Education-community and the business -community.

Dr. Sibram Nisonko

TABLE OF CONTENTS

CHAPTER NO	CONTENT	PAGE NO
1	THE ACHIEVING	9

	CEO	
2	QUALITIES OF HUMAN RESOURCES	38
3	ORGANIZATIONAL CULTURE FOR PRODUCTIVITY	43
4	MANAGEMENT OF CHANGE	46
5	QUALITY OF WORKLIFE	63

6	LEARNING WHILE DOING	105
7	THE BUCK STOPS HERE	112
8	THINKS AND ACTS LIKE A CEO	116
9	THE INTEGRATION	131

CHAPTER 1

THE ACHIEVING CEO

Society creates Institutions for its growth and development. These Institutions are the agents of change in the path of its progress. The agents of change identified by civilized societies so far are Law, Education, Ethics and Business. Business leaders are called as Chief Executive Officer (

CEO), Manager, Director or Executive. They are actually the modern rulers of people.

ROLE AND RESPONSIBILITIES OF A CEO

Commonly a COE seems to be focusing on the textbook definition of his roles. They are:

1. Managing operations
2. Ensuring profitability
3. Communicating with share holders, government and the public

4. Evolving business strategy

5. Developing and implements the vision and mission of the business enterprise.

6. Evaluating the performance of other executives

7. Keeping in touch with the latest developments in business and marketing opportunities

8. Ensuring social responsibilities

This is thoroughly materialistic way of defining the role of a CEO. The role envisaged in these functions limits his role as it neither focuses on the talents of people who work for him nor does it acknowledge the CEO's talents and achievements. Thus the above list reduces him to be an ordinary functionary, a cog in the wheel rather than an Achiever. His freedom, dignity and self-worth are stunted.

MAKING OF A CHIEF EXECUTIVE OFFICE

Human resources assessment and development has to start from the top and a CEO who can't think about his own qualities can't think of qualities of other employees. Given freedom most people can talk about what a CEO should not do but it is difficult for any insider to verbalize what an excellent CEO can do because in general Chief Executive Officers are not well groomed. They themselves feel that it is below their dignity to think of their development and nobody on earth can dare to openly talk to them about their need for development. They are either installed by the government, selection committees or powerful king makers called bosses. It seems a paradox that anybody in a growing organization feels contented that he has enough talents and he is beyond any further improvement.

WHY CEO DEVELOPMENT PROGRAM

A CEO can easily improve a deteriorated land or dysfunctional machinery. Similarly money can be arranged from various sources available today.

But what can't be recovered are the vital resources of an organization called human resources once it is deteriorated. When unprepared or ill-motivated labor fails to support the CEO all these resources will be destroyed in a short time bringing an end to the newly born factory. A lazy, dull, selfish labor is more harmful than any other poisonous thing we can think of. What gives life and strength to these unwieldy resources is the energy and dedication of a well developed human resources at the origin of which lies an excellent human resources management. A CEO, with his power over the human resources can generate flavor, beauty, music, light and life in a wasteland.

RIGHT MAN FOR THE RIGHT JOB

It is the CEO who builds an initial team of performing executives. He can start with project of selecting his team that matches with his values and thinking. This is a lifetime opportunity one can 't afford to miss. He takes charge of an organization with an initial task of building a performing culture and a performing team. When this habit-grove is broken even a lifetime effort later can't change their culture. The focus at this stage has to be on appearance, discussion manners and styles of interaction with each other. Similarly he has to build the style of employee interaction with customers, setting goals for groups and individuals, customer orientation, faith on self, productivity orientation, quality of product, discipline and team work.

Employees, customers, organizers, managers, and suppliers are eager to get associated with the enterprise with the hope that these new forms of organizations will serve the interests of all of them. This dream of the contributors can only be realized when the organization makes an earnest effort to be responsive and humanized itself. Here lies the responsibility of a professional CEO to prepare him psychologically so that his activities don't remain at the superficial level of nuts-and- bolts management. He has a greater responsibility of understanding all day-to-day problems of employees of the organization of which he is a part, search for their causes in a scientific manner and try to find a human solution to all. While doing this he studies the principles of psychology applicable in the manufacturing and commercial work environment and applies them honestly. While doing this he serves the interest of the business organizers and the other partners.

QUALITIES OF A CEO

A CEO has to inspire his employees and be a role model. It is possible when he is healthy, comfortable at work, participates in all major activities of the organization and be able to make some contribution towards that participation. He has to show maturity at work by putting emphasis on higher order needs and keeping his lower order needs subservient to these higher order needs. He shows flexibility in fulfilling his needs. He uses creativity and takes extra responsibility in achieving group tasks. He keeps his energy at more than average level in office or workshop.

THE BEGINNING

The CEO ,on probation, jump- starts with where the shoe pinches . It is anybody's guess as to what are the perennial issues that cause head ache to any new CEO. The issues are inter-group and infra-group conflicts, induction of new employees, employees' grievances, challenges of interest groups, Industrial relations, outside interference including those of politicians , employees' engagement and quality of work life.

BASIC HRD QUESTION

Why does a CEO behave in a non-human way while a sudden crises appears before him? Does he behave the same way as an ordinary worker or a daily wager normally behaves in such a circumstance. Is the animal instinct of man universal, irrespective of status, position or responsibility? Whether education and culture or even civilization has any impact on behavior of individuals in crisis.

ANIMAL INSTISTINC

Designations don't change basic instinct of man.

Animal instinct is inherent in every man. This instinct is given to any man for his survival. It appears in the forms of drive for self-preservation, an urge to procreate for which he seeks opposite sex and a desire to be in one's social group. A tiger is a tiger due to this genetic make up. A man can't be far off this instinct as long as a genetic mutation does not take place. In presence of such an instinct a man does not take rest till his desire is fulfilled or the prey is totally destructed. A socially trained man finally expresses these in the form of pleasure seeking behavior. His primary goal in all his activities is to have personal satisfaction at any cost.

PLEASURE SEEKING BEHAVIOR

The pleasure seeking behavior in an executive can be found in the form of seeking an adventurous run up, amassing more power, wealth and recognition. Socialization transforms these needs into behavior that are socially acceptable. Some of them may also be skin-deep and deceptive.

SOCIALIZATION

Executives improve their common human instinct by passing through various educational processes. Basic behavior to love or hate is learned from family culture or in a family-like culture.

Executives continue the beliefs and values on male-female relations, value of family, traditions and practices that they learned in childhood from their religion. Training by professional institutions has great influence on their style of management. Thoughts on various economic systems like capitalism and socialism influence one's behavior. Similarly the penal system teaches one autocracy, tolerance or liberalism. In modern time media also has trespassed into every phase of one's life and powerfully influences one's behavior. including those of the business leaders.

Psychologically individuals are classified as Introverts or Extroverts. Introverts have potential to use variety of learning techniques and skills required to be a better achiever. They remain more individualistic than extroverts. They are growth-oriented, more self-aware .

Extroverts tend to develop positive feelings after socialization and have positive self-concept. A successful CEO needs to maintain a balance between the two. Experience and experimentation are the powerful tools of education for adults.

ACTION PROGRAM

An educated CEO generally keeps an educated HR Manager by his side to provide strength in the operating functions of employee resources management.

EXCELLENCE IN MANAGEMENT

He uses basically a science of Human Psychology with the help of an expert in that field. In that respect any body and everybody gets attracted towards the position of a CEO with the hope that he will enjoy all the privileges of a CHIEF. Consequently he remains as a failure due to his inability to take the heavy responsibilities of that field. Just like moon there is a brighter side and a darker side having a lot of crates, cliffs and falls which can be crossed only by an expert in the principles of human psychology because a CEO is essentially a leader of a talent pool.

How to separate seeds from weeds is our basic concern of a researcher in developing a CEO. Excellence in Management occurs when the role giving matches with role taking while this process remains very complex due to the fact the role taker is one but the role givers are many. That, accordingly leads us to the point that the Head of an Organization has to have a personality *of unitas multiplex* covering right emotions, right skills and right knowledge.

An Excellent Manager is basically a healthy person with essential professional virtues. He loves his job, continuously develops his skills, takes initiative in spite of all unfavorable circumstances and feels capable to perform his duties in all situations. He carries on his duties hopefully and completes responsibilities with total trust on people. He accepts his role willingly. He never reduces his willingness and energy in fulfilling his role, his main focus being their growth and development of employees. A boss has to avoid all types of prejudices ranging from biased attitudes, opinions, to those against certain race, gender, color, religion or region.

WORKING WITH DATA

He uses research technique; analyses data honestly and scientifically, evaluates them and finally conveys to the workers honestly and helps them to find solutions to their work related problems. Here he need to be rational and logical, avoids being impulsive.

SOLVING EMPLOYEES' PROBLEMS

It is essential for a leader to be able to help his team members to be calm in crises, look at data causing problems and then try to find a workable solution together. The leader here is supportive and facilitative.

PERSUASIVENESS

When the manager is very well convinced about something, he has a duty to remove resistance and to work for smooth functioning of the idea. He uses feelings, information and reasons to convince the user to act upon team.

ABILITY TO WORK IN A TEAM

He understands the goals and converts them in the way his workers can understand them. He conveys them in simple language. He follows a common approach and makes each accountable for the result. He remains an active partner at each stage of working, not giving any one a feeling of inferiority or superiority.

TAKING INITIATIVE

The new generation CEO is a different being. With the change in environment he has to change his role and responsibilities. He has to be a manger, a leader and a developer. He has to work more with workers than the traditional CEO does. He has to be more relation oriented than task oriented. He needs to act pro-actively in predicting the expectations of the new age workers. He needs to learn many new skills in order to guide the knowledge workers today. He makes self-assessment of his abilities and skills by continuously collecting feedback from his team members.

He gets himself ready to meet new challenges and avail opportunities .He actively participated in discussions and sharing ideas with his colleagues regarding how the tools, systems, materials and processes man be improved.

LEADING BY EXAMPLES

The CEO needs to respect knowledge. He may listen to what the juniors say and learn from them. He needs to get involved in actual work. It will also boost morale of workers. When the managers join hands with workers the workers in turn will learn to help others. By being in touch with the basic work at plant level he can earn the reputation of a manager of the people and a manager –in – need.

ACCEPTANCE

He considers every employee of his unit of business as an important source of talent and a vital resource for his business, by accepting all their differences on the basis of color, caste, race etc. Performance and talents in use are more productive than selection of people of high caste or men of blue blood or descendants of warier race.

ABILITY TO LEARN

For a CEO the universe is his house. Any day or any time he may face a surprise. In spite of high-level of scientific preparations things may go hay way. He needs to learn to be witty and quick in sensing the situation. His ability to get quick answers is his ability to learn. When he learns from his juniors' work and from adversaries and from adverse situations he develops his ability to learn.

KNOWLEDGE

When he reads the books and journals relating to his business his knowledge- base increases .He has to be a well -read man by choice. His choice of subjects is very wide and he uses analogies, inferences and comparisons to get insights for his field of work.

RESOURCEFULNESS

He shows his resourcefulness by helping others to cope

with difficult situations. He helps them to make old things work better. He helps them to work more effectively and imaginatively.

EMTIONAL MATURITY

He understands the reasons for others emotions and his own emotions. He then manages his own emotions so that the emotions of his employees don't affect their performance.

CREATIVITY

He gives new solutions to old problems. Similarly he helps them use new methods of working more economically in reduced time.

INNOVATIVENESS

He helps his juniors to work faster, better and smarter ways of working.

ADOPTABILITY

Things may not be available the way an employee wants. The manager or the CEO inspires his team members to change and work under new situation and new information.

TEAM BUILDING

He helps workers to work together, in collaboration with

each other and in supportive manner. He develops systems of delegation, communication and suggestions to improve teamwork.

INVENTORY OF SKILLS

The level of development can be assessed with an instrument to measure the skills and abilities and behavioral sensitivity of a CEO. At the lowest rung lays his technical skills and at the highest level is his skills to handle HRD techniques for workers.

The issues that have remained unattended so far are freedom, dignity and self-worth of workers, developing autonomous work group, quality of work life of workers, development of skills required for growth of workers .In this case some common techniques are job rotation, Job redesign, job enrichment, job enlargement, democracy at work.

People generally compare the value of their own with those of others in similar work situations based on their inputs and outputs. Everybody wants to be treated equally and fairly. Pains in the heart are deeper due to perceived unfairness at work. This feeling - real or imaginary- requires to be removed early.

MANAGEMENT BIASES

From the beginning of his career a CEO might have come across many coworkers who have had helped him, supported him and even encouraged him. It is rational not to forget such small helps and supports. One should not forget them as one grows in the ladder. During crises, bad times and good times, ups and downs, during happy time and distressful time only our near workers come to our rescue. While taking charge of his own development a CEO assigns maximum value to establishing relationship with workers, as they are his assets and the asset builders of the company. It means providing support, encouragement and guiding them in the developmental path is a human approach. There are many workers who look to the boss as their god and savior.

A supervisor can't overlook the performance of subordinates. A CEO has to maintain a record of all the contributions that a worker makes and converts them into monitory form and then examines how the worker needs his support during his difficulties. All performances are the product of sincere efforts of dedicated workers. How can their contribution be taken casually or overlooked in order to gain a little personal benefit? He has to avoid showing extra attention to people who take additional pains to gain the favor of bosses. He has to avoid all those who have negative intentions, attitudes and behavior. Ants may hover around you as long as you are covered with sugar. What happens when sugar stock comes to an end. Selfish relations don't last long. There are many silent workers. They only know how to work and serve. They don't demand anything openly because they have total trust on their superior. Not recognizing good performance is definitely demoralizing. In order to avoid extra efforts bosses make clustering or group them into average performers. This is harmful to the organization.

It is dangerous to try to take revenge for a head of the organization.t is a costly exercise that never gets you anywhere. The Head of an organization has a special responsibility of growing above any prejudices ranging from attitudes, opinions, race, gender, age, religion to skin color. A persons contribution is the sum total of his efforts, energy and application of skills at work. One has to avoid decisions on the basis of recent events.

There need to be separate systems for development and for rewards. More rigorous application of analysis techniques and recording events are required to link assessment of a manager with rewards.

A GROWTH ORIENTED EXECUTIVE

Social development being the final aim of any social activity including business, a matured head of a business organization is committed to its people , his workers, both physically and intellectually. Not only he tries for their growth but he also inspires his team members to work for the worker' development. For achieving this broad aim he tries to establish a socially conducive environment around the business enterprise.

A growth oriented CEO while caring for his growth sees growth of his workers as the vital factor for his growth.

Just like a physician always keeps his mind on his patients, a musician on his music and a painter on his pant this cadre of CEO never keeps his worker's interests away from his mind.

He reaches his destination by invoking the talent of the people. Sensual attachment or actions with selfish desires may give some quick results . But in the long run they will only give you pains. His raises his duties towards workers from prescribed to benevolent and from benevolent to supportive . He stills rises to be motivational leader from being an ordinary manager. His level of satisfaction rises to the peak when people regard him as an Achieving CEO who also develops his associates and subordinates.

In the heart of all these activities should lay a noble humanitarian desire , a desire to achieve the welfare of the wider society. May be the joy he sees in the achievement of his worker is his real achievement.

He goes beyond his own ego and shows all the finer virtues of a close friend, a wise seer and a learned guide. He needs to regain his freedom by breaking the shackles of being a center of power, a selfish corporate being or a man with belly full of greediness, anger and hate.

The executive is as much comfortable with himself as with his workers. When he decides to disagree with any body he never tries to enforce his views. On the contrary, before jumping into any conclusion, he asks for the reasons behind the other views, finds facts and justifications. He uses his reason and logic for his disagreements in an unbiased way. He even tries to get into the other's shoes while evaluating the views.

He improves the evaluation of an important suggestion from a worker by even taking the help of a third uninvolved party or an impartial body or group. He shows openness, honesty and trust. He is cooperative. He does not display anger, disdain or disgust. He is hopeful even in adverse positions, when his decisions are questioned.

Even when coming to a conclusion that goes against a worker he first shares his positive views and then he gives his decision giving reasons . In the process he takes care not to create a feeling of failure or low self –esteem in the mind of the workers. He also avoids by showing any sign of superior feeling that he has defeated his workers since their loss is in fact his own loss. He acknowledges others being better in certain ways and allows them to work on that line and in that process he tries to build their confidence. He thoroughly searches various ways and means to appreciate the knowledge , skills and attitudes of workers.

In failures he does not indulge in blaming behavior or searching for a scape-goat .On the contrary he goes for self-reflection aiming at his own improvement as a well as at the improvement of his workers.

HRD PROCESS FOR THE CEO

1. IDENTIFICATION OF FORCES IN ROLE ENVIRONMENT ;

2. LISTING OF ABILITIES, KNOWLEDGE, SKILLS, ATTITUDES AND ATTRIBUTES (LITERATURE SURVEY);

3. PRILIMINARY SURVEY BY INTERESTED ROLE SENDERS LINKING WITH THE PRILIMINARY SURVEY;

4. COLLECTION OF PERFORMANCE RATINGS OF

LAST THREE YEARS;

5. ASSESSMENT OF ABILITIES THROUGH PSYCHOLOGICAL TESTS/INSTRUMENTS ;

6. STATISTICAL ANALYSIS FOLLOWED BY AN EXERCISE OF CORRELATION OF PERFORMANCE WITH ABILITIES;

7. CONCLUSION ON QUALITIES OF CEOs.

8. DESIGNING OF ASSESSMENT SYSTEM .

9. EVOLVING OF DEVELOPMENT STRATEGIES - MENTORING , SENSITIVITY TRAINING,TEAM BUILDING ,BEHAVIORAL MODIFICATION TECHNIQUES AND SKILLS DEVELOPMENT

TECHNIQUES

CHAPTER 2

QUALITY OF HUMAN RESOURCES

In order to find the quality of a business, people generally measure the quality of human resources of that business. These human resources include their workers, supervisors and managers. In fact designations don't matter. What matters are the culture of the organization, competencies of human resources and the communication skills of the employees including managers. The strength of the CEO is the strength of the lowest rung employees of the company since they are the point of first contact for anybody outside the business. They are , in fact ,the business. Take it or leave it.

The CEO is the catalyst in creating such an opener. He invites them, lives with them and builds them from the root. Let us remember the hard truth that pearls are never available on a tree or on a dressing table . They are collected from a deep sea after diving down in an abysmal ocean. The diver's own behavior matters everything.

The Achieving CEO tries to read and understand his behavior by studying the principles of psychology. It will help him to describe, explain , study and understand his behavior including those of others in a scientific manner. That will help him to predict and control behavior for better quality of work.

The new age executives look at their employees as future-ready executives. They develop their enabling capabilities to meet any unforeseen future challenges. They develop their process capabilities in decision-making. As an experiment they provide new tasks, delegate significant responsibilities, allow employees to decide on their work related matters and allow them to use any fair technique to achieve their goals.

Besides the CEO discusses with each executive to identify key competencies required for effective performance of their jobs. This process starts with :

- λ Business plan ,strategies and objectives

- λ Analysis of role responsibilities

- λ Customer requirements

- λ Future requirements on the basis of predictions of industry wide changes.

- λ Identifying capabilities for each role on the basis of future changes. These capabilities center on strategies, problem solving, decision-making, time management, stress management, creativity and communication.

- λ Preparing executives to undertake similar exercises for their subordinates.

As against expectations on the basis of job demands we need to assess the existing skills and competencies of employees on role. It has to be followed by a comparative analysis between the two lists and preparing a deficiency-list. Here lies the link between HRD for CEO with the HRD for the employees. The goal of HRD efforts by the

CEO is to remove the gap and make the employees competent so that his journey for achievement can take off.

CHAPTER 3

ORGANIZATIONAL CULTURE FOR PRODUCTIVITY

Culture is the most important strength of an organization. The work progress of a CEO can either be smooth or tough depending upon the cultural – foundation of the organization. The achieving CEO keeps this on focus before any other act of development. The first step is to make a measurement of the existing culture of the organization. This could be done by a cross-sectional survey of employees. This survey is to find out the levels of satisfaction of employees, their level of involvement in the organization and the hidden ailments in the organization and management. The survey may have various elements some of which are identified below:

- ❖ Survey of leadership style.

- ❖ Survey of supervisory attitudes and behavior.

- ❖ Survey of psychological processes like trust, values, communication and conflict management.

- ❖ Survey of effective organizational structure and technology.

A powerful approach to bring about organizational change is to start with the higher levels of management. It means a top-down approach. It may seem easy to change organizational culture on paper; it is ,in fact, very difficult in practice as the greatest hurdles are the top executives. Change in performance is easier when it starts with change in the values of the managers. The CEO needs to change the work process and daily practices of the executive team. He keeps himself involved for some time on daily basis on such process. He can help them achieve their key performance areas better by having joint sessions on goal clarifications. Organizational communications get strengthened when inter-group and inter personal communications improve.

He needs to educate his team, initially, to focus on goals not means since the later are within his control. The managers, in turn, need to get the pulse of the business partners, suppliers and the customers. There needs to be a strong team approach in order to achieve customer satisfaction.

CHAPTER 4

MANAGEMENT OF CHANGE

INJECTION OF QUALITY INTO TIME

The story of tortoise and the hare is very educative for thinkers on the subject. It is better to be smart, proactive and bold instead of lazy, dull and inactive. An achieving executive works smart not more.

It is not essential for a CEO to mark his attendance through a punch card or biometric attendance system. His presence has to be felt by his role senders, namely employees, customers, managers, board members and suppliers. He injects quality in every dealings and in every minute he spends time with them. The spirit of quality in him is the one that inspires his followers and all the above groups who have volunteered to be associated with him. To start with, this may seem to be a herculean task but he commits to manage the change.

CONFLICT RESOLUTION

The CEO manages many conflicts between technological requirement and human requirements. Following ergonomics helps him initially. Next comes maintenance of mechanical speed which is taken care of by modern safety measures and techniques. More difficult part is to handle group morale along with maintenance of efficiency. Zeal, enthusiasm, energy, positive feelings and loyalty are the results of good team morale. It is ensured by the supervisory behavior, job matching one's skills, job enrichment, rewards matching efforts and results.

EMPLOYEE INDUCTION

Inducting new employees into an organization starts with good first day experience and socialization. The induction program may consist of introducing him to people who matter in the company, company details including its history, culture and business, job details, introducing work team, details of facilities and privileges. The emphasis is more on relationships, style of interaction, traditions and values.

GRIEVANCES

A small grievance of a disgruntled employee may spread the dissatisfaction like a wild fire since unhappiness spreads faster than happiness.

Time bound, action oriented written procedure of grievance redressing needs to be evolved. A properly framed system consisting of a form of presentation of grievances, an identified body to handle the system, opportunity for personal representation and a choice for appeal may create confidence of the people in the system. There has to be a time-bound action program. The CEO has to ensure all these.

INTEREST GROUPS

A big business is a big place for people to pursue their personal interests. Workers may form cultural groups, trade union groups and also welfare groups. In a democratic society all these associations are allowed ,provided they don't hamper the primary goal of the organization.

The CEO keeps himself updated with status reports periodically. He also shows interest in these activities in the role of a well wisher and a guide. This proactive step may encourage the involved people to maintain the required limit.

EMPLOYEE EXIT

Periodically employees may retire or even resign. Every employee - exit is taken an opportunity to obtain a frank feedback about the organization, systems and people.

SUGGESTIONS

Employees are given ample opportunities to avail the suggestion system of the company to share and exchange company related topics like production, productivity, rewards , recognition, employee welfare, systems and procedure of administration . Workers are the owners of the practical experiences at the grass root level. Hence seeking their suggestion on any topic of management may add value of being practical. It has to be formally and actively administered by a specific committee of expert -employees .Visibility of the system ,timely response to suggestions and rewards and actions are the important elements to make it a success.

LAW AND INDUSTRIAL RELATIONS

Workers and unions require recognition . They also require justice and fair play .The CEO ensures their participation in certain structured systems and committees .In order to settle disputes a well-written procedure with principles of collective bargaining is evolved.

GOVERNMENT CONTROL

Industrial relations become an internal matter of company when the management treats the workers as equal partners. The CEO and his team of management avoid all litigations and use of legal machinery as far as possible. Instead, they need to settle disputes with bilateral understanding with the spirit of partnership.

Labor welfare activities are essential for physical and mental well being of workers. Workers express their dissatisfaction when anything is imposed on them without consultation. It is essential that all welfare systems and schemes are to be left to committees of workers .There can be various functional committees on canteen, child welfare, woman welfare, hospital facilities, transport and housing.

Employee Turnover statistics provides vital

information about ailments in the company. They may relate to supervisory competencies, work design , wages system or industrial relations.

Workers' Participation helps in management of people. This type of worker engagement mechanism can be facilitated by seeking their commitment on production related projects, seeking acceptance of projects of change . Participation of workers is very vital on matters of employee development and use of talents .It reduces the blindness of the top managers towards work related tools and techniques .

Reward and compensation is a subject of most

controversies in industries .All disputes with workers mostly center around this topic. A CEO has to look after the equity element in compensation. Similar level jobs are to be paid about the same compensation t means bigger jobs are paid more than smaller jobs. Using industry and region specific market data on compensations are to be fixed to avoid feeling of unfair worker compensation.

The CEO of a company that produces quality - products , besides getting better financial rewards, gets high reputation in the market as well as among colleagues. Quality control plays a significant role in the functioning of a CEO.

Most high performing executives have the habit of riding over others while focusing on their task performance. This results in employee negligence leading to low morale of employees. It may finally end in worker frustration and agitation. It requires personal touch and counseling. Similarly ,it is advisable to use Counseling Skills while handling slow performers, instead of rejecting the worker.

It is the responsibility of a CEO to change and lead a non-performing bunch of common men who have their eyes fixed on their basic wants into a high achieving men - these men may range from workers to managers. A CEO has to take charge of his emotions and attitudes along with skills, competencies and behavior. An Achieving CEO studies the values and mission statements of the organization that he leads. His main task is to develop a workable organizational vision and philosophy, Then he seeks the help of his team members to develop the statements of values and beliefs that can energize them. He helps the team to develop a positive style of interaction, a productive organizational structure, a workable business strategy, plans of action, systems and infrastructure.

PROFESSIONAL APPROACH

Professional approach to Quality of work life generally directs the CEO's energy on people. He perceives things on the basis of facts and clarity of information. His thoughts are objective and detached. His judgments are structured and predictable. For the new generation CEO the present organizational principles pose a very big hurdle. He needs to develop an organic team fussing on teamwork rather than a division of work .In this process workers have to complement each other instead of duplicating. Instead of individual responsibility and authority the CEO ensures balancing of authority and responsibility. Too much of discipline and enforcement of rulebook may cause harm to a growing organization since sometimes talented workers are found to be eccentric. It is imperative for achieving excellence in Human resources management to delegate responsibility. At the same time responsibility has to be matched with authority. Any body to be an achiever is to have unity of direction. At the same time direction, goal and vision can't be textual .They all have to be evolved with general participation by the employees in order to be appropriate and actionable.

CONFLICTS IN DEVELOPMENT

In organizations one can come across various types of conflicts .Depending upon responsibilities people may get different levels of salary and enjoy various perks. Efforts are required to be made in such a manner that workers don't develop a feeling of lowliness or insignificance. Any such situation should be nipped at the bud. Authority should be widely distributed in order to avoid autocratic behavior. Employees are to be free from external politics. Knowledge and skills are not to be utilized as a source of power. They are to be made an asset for the team. Trade unions should no be allowed to grow as an alternative to management ,a balancing organization or center of power. They are better when they grow as a partner of management. Rewarding and punishing power may be assigned to a well trained committee of workers and supervisors to avoid any feeling of unfair treatment.

It is not unknown to any body that a cashier manages cash and the store-keeper manages the store. There is nothing special for a Chief Executive Officer to manage any of these things when the functionaries manage the functions. The only thing left for the Head is to facilitate their function and strengthen their skills. The CEO who can't be close to the workers and who can't develop them is no better than a destroyer of business; in fact it will not take much time for such unit to get deteriorated. The signing top of a tree is the symbol of its health.

FACILITATOR

The Chief has to start with the assessment of skills and knowledge in his business and also to find whether the operators are aware of the latest developments. It is imperative that he develops a habit of updating his knowledge on a continuous basis.

The power of a wheel is definitely greater than the sum total of the powers of the cogs. The Chief sees the organization as a pyramid of teams not individuals. Team spirit could be as much destructive as productive. The CEO has to start with development vision for the organization, which has to be a participation- process in order to facilitate implementation. Once it is evolved and finalized and written down the process of implementation starts with communication down to every level including the trade unions and customers. Feedback ,if any received has to be responded , deliberated and acted upon in a positive manner, quickly and responsibly.

The process of downward communication has to synchronize with facilitating techniques for upward communication. The team that looks after policy has to consist of people with complementary skills and those with higher order needs. Team formation is successful when it has started seeing a big picture. Conflicts when rises require quick resolution with focus on team development. The foundation for such a team is built by a productive culture wherein people are willing to take responsibility and are working with commitment to the set goals with out expecting quick fruits of action. The evidence lies in the risk taking behavior and feeling of team identity. It is followed by feelings of mutual warmth and support. Team is delegated with adequate power to be able to take informed intelligent decision. Needless to say that the culture of CEO goes a long way to shape the work climate .It includes the way he responds to technology and people, language of his interaction and his priorities in work life.

Only a capable leader can develop a team. Such leader has the capacity to motivate and energize people around them. He doesn't wait for opportunities but creates opportunities. He is open to challenges, has ability to keep cool even in adverse circumstances. He perceives good in every aspect of life. His language is positive. He follows a self-stimulating life-style. He loves people and all social activities although he may not be directly involved all those activities. He leads a satisfying family life. He has no grudges or grumblings but has beliefs on a broader vision of life .

He takes feedback from workers' work experiences and redesigns work in such a manner that they get variety , learning experience, find meaning and social recognition in work . All these efforts are so structured at the beginning itself so that the relationship between workers and the management starts developing on positive lines from the beginning .It is the first impression that lasts long.

CRISES MANAGEMENT

The recent developments in business and industry

are a sad reflection on the quality of HRM. Researchers of HRM are depressed by the way the industrial workers are treated on the face of pandemic. How many of them are laid off, retrenched, even dismissed nobody knows. Very sadly they are allowed to fend for themselves on the face of a crisis as they are treated like orphan children and nobody has shown any sense of responsibility for the life of workers and their families.

This behavior of Management is an eye opener for all researchers in the field of HRD. The data when collected authentically will help us know their thoughts, feelings, actions and goals. That will help us find cause of unhealthy behavior of CEOs.

The immediate hurdle to understand is the CEO's arguments and thoughts . When workers are distressed due to crisis the CEO can't take it lightly as a deviation of behavior. It actually reflects the climate of HRD in organizations since most organizations have shown such a behavior. This will also make us alert about how the CEOs will react when faced with any other crisis in future. The devastating situation of the present day workers force any thinker to think loudly about the need for HRD for the CEOs and his colleagues. Workers can work only as long as managers manage.

CHAPTER 5

QUALITY OF WORKLIFE

Quality of work life (QWL) is an essential part of Human Resources Development (HRD) for a CEO. QWL starts from the top and a CEO who can't think about his own life , can't think of life of workers. Given freedom most people can talk about what a CEO should not do but it is difficult to verbalize what an excellent CEO can do because in general Chief Executive Officers are not well groomed since they feel it is below their dignity to think of their development and nobody on earth can dare to openly talk to them about their development. They are either installed by the government, selection committees or powerful king makers called bosses. Then they assume to be all -in –all .

WHY CEO DEVELOPMENT PROGRAM

A CEO can easily improve a deteriorated land or dysfunctional machinery. Similarly money can be arranged from various sources available today.

But what can't be recovered is the vital resource called human resources once it is deteriorated. When unprepared or ill-motivated labor fails to support the CEO all these resources will be destroyed in a short time bringing an end to the newly born factory. A lazy, dull, selfish labor is more harmful than any other poisonous thing we can think of. What gives life and strength to these unwieldy resources is the energy and dedication of a well developed human resources at the origin of which lies an excellent Human Resources Management. A CEO, with his power over the human resources can generate flavor, beauty, music, light and life in a wasteland.

RIGHT MAN FOR THE RIGHT JOB

It is the CEO who builds an initial team of performing executives. He can start with project of selecting his team that matches with his values and thinking. This is a lifetime opportunity one can't afford to miss. He takes the charge of an organization with an initial task of building a performing culture and a performing team. This habit-grove is broken even a lifetime effort later can't change their culture. The focus at this stage has to be on appearance, table manners and styles of interaction with each other. Similarly he has to build the style of employee interaction with customers, setting goals for groups and individuals, customer orientation, faith on self, productivity orientation, quality of product, discipline and team work.

Business and commercial organizations are allowed to organize and grow by the society with the hope that these new forms of organizations will serve the interests of the society at large. This dream of the society can only be realized when the organizations make an earnest effort to humanize itself. Here lies the responsibility of a professional CEO to prepare him psychologically so that his activities don't remain at the superficial level of nuts-and- bolts management ; the management that has eyes on the cash-box is not definitely the management of the millennium .Today's management has to go far deeper into the problem and also has knowledge of prediction quite in advance of time . He has a greater responsibility of understanding all day-to-day problems of employees of the organization of which he is a part, searching for their causes in a scientific manner and trying to find a human solution to all in a sustainable manner. While doing this he studies all the principles of psychology applicable in a manufacturing and commercial work environment and applies them honestly.

PERSONALITY OF A CEO

A CEO has to inspire his employees and be a role model. It is possible when he is healthy, comfortable at work. He participates in all major activities of the organization and is able to make some contribution towards every matter that comes to his notice. He has to show maturity at work by putting emphasis on higher order needs and keeping his lower order needs subservient to these higher order needs. He shows flexibility in fulfilling his needs. He uses creativity and takes extra responsibility in achieving group tasks. He keeps his energy at more than average level in office or workshop.

An educated CEO generally keeps an educated HR Manager by his side to provide strength in the operating functions of employee resources management. On the contrary one who alienates the HRD manager is definitely a poisonous plant or a deadwood.

EXCELLENCE IN MANAGEMENT

He uses basically a science of Human Psychology with the help of an expert in that field. In that respect any body and everybody gets attracted towards the position of a CEO with the hope that he will enjoy all the privileges of a CHIEF. Consequently he remains as a failure due to his inability to take the heavy responsibilities of that field. Just like moon there is a brighter side and a darker side having a lot of crates, cliffs and falls which can be crossed only by an expert in the principles of human psychology because a CEO is essentially a leader of a talent pool.

How to identifying seeds from weeds is our basic concern of a researcher in developing a CEO. Excellence- in - Management occurs when the role giving matches with role taking while this process remains very complex due to the fact the role taker is one but the role givers are many. That, accordingly leads us to the point that the Head of an Organization has to have a personality *of unitas multiplex* covering right emotions, right skills and right knowledge.

An Excellent HR Manager is a basically a healthy person with essential professional virtues. He loves his job, continuously develops his skills, takes initiative in spite of all unfavorable circumstances and feels capable to perform his duties in all situations. He carries on his duties hopefully and completes responsibilities with total trust on people. He accepts his role willingly. He never reduces his willingness and energy in fulfilling his role, removing constraints at work and facilitating the growth and development of employees.

PROCESS OF DEVELOPMENT

A worker gets into a work atmosphere with an imaginary hope that all his dreamy wishes will be fulfilled. Once inside the productive organization he looks for development and in the process he seeks the support of the bosses to chalk out a career course in order to achieve what lies dormant in his mind. He starts working hard and seriously learns all the skills, both common and exceptional.

CHALLENGES IN THE PROCESS OF DEVELOPMENT

CONFLICT RESOLUTION

The CEO manages many conflicts between technological requirement and human requirements. Following ergonomics helps him initially. Next comes maintenance of mechanical speed, which is taken care of, by modern safety measures and techniques. More difficult part is to handle group morale along maintenance of efficiency. Zeal, enthusiasm, energy, positive feelings and loyalty are the results of good team morale. It is ensured by the supervisory behavior, job matching one's skills, job enrichment, rewards matching efforts and results.

INDUCTION OF NEW EMPLOYEES

Integrating new employees into an organization starts with good first day experience and socialization. The induction program consists of introducing with people he has to work with, company details including its history, culture and business, job details, introducing work team, details of facilities and privileges. The emphasis is more on relationships, style of interaction, traditions and values.

Grievances

A time bound, action oriented written procedure of grievance redressal is followed.

Interest groups. The CEO keeps himself updated with status reports periodically.

EMPLOYEE EXIT

Every employee exit is taken an opportunity to obtain a frank feedback about the employees on retirement, resignation etc.

SUGGESTION SYSTEM

Every employee can be given opportunity to avail the suggestion system of the company to share and exchange company related topics like production, productivity, rewards, recognition, employee welfare systems and procedure of administration. The top management can seek views of other on topics suggested by the management. It is administered by a specific committee of expert -employees.

VISIBILITY OF THE SYSTEM

Care need to be given at the designing stage. The scheme may consist of all details that may encourage employees to participate in large numbers .The elements may consist of identification of probable subjects, elements of the presented idea, tools and techniques of implementation, people to be involved , benefits to be accrued etc.

In order to develop trust of the people the scheme should have methods of recognition and rewards.

LAW AND INDUSTRIAL RELATIONS

Workers and unions require recognition .The CEO ensures their participation in all structured systems and committees

.In order to settle disputes a well written procedure with principles of collective bargaining is evolved.

SPIRIT OF PARTNERSHIP

Industrial relations become an internal matter of the company when the management treats the workers as equal partners. The CEO and his team of management avoid all litigations and use of legal machineries as far as possible .Instead ,they need to settle all disputes with bilateral understanding, that is with the spirit of partnership. Spirit of litigation has to be avoided at any cost . The initiation has to come from the management. It is better to show extra favor towards a worker when in confusion while interpreting the rules applicable to him, instead of going to a court of law for getting decisions favorable to the management. This will have a lasting impact on their bilateral relations.

Labor welfare activities are essential for physical and mental wellbeing of workers. Workers express their dissatisfaction when anything is imposed on them without consultation.it is essential that all welfare systems and schemes are to be left to committees of workers .There can be various functional committees on canteen, child welfare, woman welfare, hospital facilities, transport and housing.

Employee Turnover statistics provides vital information about ailments in the company.

Workers' Participation helps in better management of people . It is facilitated if managers take steps to seek their commitment on existing projects , requesting acceptance of new projects, using talents of workers in implementation.

Rewards and compensations are subjects of most controversies in Industries . Many disputes with workers center on this topic. A CEO has to look after the equity element in compensation. Similar level jobs are to be paid about the same compensation .It means bigger jobs are paid more than smaller jobs. CEOs use industry and region specific market data before compensation systems are finalized . Workers are given opportunities to participate in discussions while finalizing the schemes.

The CEO of a company that produces quality -product , besides getting better financial rewards, gets high reputation in the market as well as among colleagues. Quality control plays a significant role in the functioning of a CEO.

Most high performing executives have the habit of riding over others while focusing on their task performance. That results in low morale of employees and causes frustration. It is advisable to use Counseling Skills wile handling slow performers.

It is the responsibility of a CEO to change attitudes of worker. His own attitudes towards workers matter the most. The needs and attitudes of the top management set the agenda for general workers. A lazy manager produces a lazy worker. Similarly an achieving leader attracts achieving workers around him like a honey bee. The team spirit of the CEO can only produce a team of high achieving men -these men may range from workers to managers.

A performing team has a COE at its head who first takes charge of his emotions and attitudes along with skills, competencies and behavior. To motivate the team it requires essentially conveying high spirit and seeking workers commitment on all that represents an excellent organization. It means developing organizational vision, philosophy, values, beliefs , style of interaction, organizational structure, business strategy, plans of action, systems ,infrastructure.

PROFESSIONAL APPROACH

Professional approach to Quality of work life generally directs the CEO's energy on people. He perceives things on the basis of facts and clarity of information. His thoughts are objective and detached. His judgments are structured and predictable. For this new generation CEO the present organizational principles pose a very big hurdle. He needs to develop an organic team fussing of team work rather than a division of work .In this process ,workers have to complement each other instead of duplicating. Instead of individual responsibility and authority the CEO ensures balancing of authority and responsibility. Too much of discipline and enforcement of rule-book may cause harm to a growing organization since sometimes talented workers are found to be eccentric. It is imperative for achieving an excellence in Human resources management to delegate responsibility. At the same time responsibility has to be matched with authority. Any body to be an achiever is to have unity of direction. At the same time direction, goal and vision can't be textual. They all have to be evolved with general participation by the worker in order to be actionable.

CONFLICTS IN DEVELOPMENT

In organizations one can come across various types of conflicts .Depending upon responsibilities people may get different levels of salary and enjoy various perks. Efforts are required to be made in such a manner that workers don't develop a feeling of lowliness or insignificance. Any such situation should be nipped at the bud. Authority should be widely distributed in order to avoid autocratic behavior. Employees are to be free from external politics. Knowledge and skills are not to be utilized as a source of power. They are to be made an asset for the team. Trade unions should no be allowed to grow as an alternative to management ,a balancing organization or center of power. They are to be developed as a partner of management. Rewarding and punishing power may be assigned to a well trained committee to avoid any unfair treatment.

ROLE OF A CEO

It is not unknown to any body that a cashier manages cash and the store-keeper manages the store. There is nothing special for a Chief Executive Officer to manage any of these things when the functionaries manage the functions. The only thing left for the Head is to facilitate their function and strengthen their skills. The CEO who can't be close to the workers and develops them is going to destroy the business within no time.

FACILITATOR

The Chief has to start with the assessment of skills and knowledge in his business and also to find whether the operators are aware of the latest development.t is imperative that he himself updates his knowledge on a continuous basis.

The power of a wheel is definitely greater than the sum total of the powers of the cogs. The Chief sees the organization as a pyramid of teams not individuals. Team spirit could be as much destructive as productive. The CEO has to start with development vision for the organization, which has to be a participative process in order to facilitate implementation. Once it is evolved and finalized and written down the process of implementation starts with communication down to every level including the trade unions and customers. Feedback ,if any received has to responded after deliberations.

The process of downward communication follows with facilitating upward communication. The team has to consist of people with complementary skills and those with higher order needs. Team formation is successful when it can see a big picture. Conflicts when arise require quick resolution with focus on team development. The foundation for such a team is built by a productive culture wherein people are willing to take responsibility and work with commitment to the set goals with out expecting quick fruits of action. The evidence lies in the risk taking behavior and feeling of team identity.it also is followed by feelings of mutual warmth and support .Team is delegated with adequate power to be able to take informed intelligent decision. Needless to say that the culture of CEO goes a long way to shape the work climate. It includes the way he responds to technology and people, language of his interaction and his priorities in work life.

Only a capable leader can develop a team. Such leader has the capacity to motivate and energize people around him .He doesn't wait for opportunities but creates opportunities. He is open to challenges, has ability to keep cool even in adverse circumstances. He perceives good in every aspect of life. His language is positive. He follows a self-stimulating life-style. He loves people and all social activities in the environment although he may not be directly involved all those activities. He leads a satisfying family life. He has no grudges or grumblings but believes on a broader vision of life.

He takes feedback from workers and their work experiences and redesigns work in such a manner that they get variety, learning experience, find meaning and social recognition in work. All these efforts are so structured at the beginning itself so that the relationship between workers and the management starts developing on positive lines from the beginning.

CRISES MANAGEMENT

The recent developments in business and industry are a sad reflection on the quality of HRM. Researchers of HRM are depressed by the way the industrial workers are treated on the face of pandemic. How many of them are laid off, retrenched, even dismissed nobody knows. Very sadly they are allowed to fend for themselves on the face of a crisis as they are treated like orphan children and nobody has shown any sense of responsibility for the life of workers and their families.

This behavior of Management is an eye opener for all researchers in the field of HRD. The data when collected authentically will help us know their thoughts, feelings, actions and goals. That will help us find cause of unhealthy behavior of CEOs.

The immediate hurdle to understanding is their reaction to a deviation .A CEO is testes for actual talent when environment changes, market condition becomes adverse workers do not behave normally, Such an adversity actually reflects the climate of HRD in organizations since most organizations have shown such a behavior. This will also make us predict about how the CEOs will react when faced with any other crisis in future.

BASIC HRD QUESTION

Why does a CEO behave in a non-human way while a sudden crises appears before him? Does he behave the same way as an ordinary worker or a daily wager normally behaves in such a circumstance. Is the animal instinct of man universal, irrespective of status, position or responsibility. Whether education and culture or even civilization has any impact on behavior of individuals in crisis.

EMOTIONAL CONSTRAINTS

ANIMAL INSTISTINC

Designations don't change basic instinct of man. Animal instinct is inherent in every man. This instinct is given to any man for his survival. It appears in the forms of drive for self preservation, an urge to procreate for which he seeks opposite sex and a desire to be in one's social group. A tiger is a tiger due to this genetic make up. A man can't be far off this instinct as long as a genetic mutation does not take place. In presence of such an instinct a man does not take rest till his desire is fulfilled or the prey is totally destructed. A socially trained man finally expresses these in the form of pleasure seeking behavior. His primary goal in all his activities is to have personal satisfaction at any cost.

PLEASURE SEEKING BEHAVIOR

The pleasure seeking behavior in an executive can be found in the form of seeking adventure, power, wealth and recognition. Socialization transforms these needs into behavior that are socially acceptable. Some of them may also be kin-deep and deceptive.

SOCIALIZATION

Executives improve their common human instinct by passing through various educational process. Basic behavior to love or hate is learned from family culture. Executives continue the beliefs and values on male-female relations, value of family, traditions and practices that they learnt in childhood from their religion. Training by professional institutions also has great influence on their style of management. Thoughts on various economic system like capitalism and socialism influence one's behavior .Similarly the penal system teaches one autocracy tolerance or liberalism . In modern time media has trespassed into every phase of one's life and powerfully influences one's behavior..

Psychologically individuals are classified as Introverts or Extraverts. Introverts have potential to used variety of learning techniques and skills required to be a better achiever. They remain more individualistic than extroverts. They are growth oriented, more self-aware .

Extroverts tend to develop positive feelings after socialization and have positive self concept. A successful CEO needs to maintain a balanced approach.

ACTION PROGRAM

An educated CEO generally keeps an educated HR Manager by his side to provide strength in the operating functions of employee resources management.

EXCELLENCE IN MANAGEMENT

He uses basically a science of Human Psychology with the help of an expert in that field. In that respect any body and everybody gets attracted towards the position of a CEO with the hope that he will enjoy all the privileges of a CHIEF. Consequently he remains as a failure due to his inability to take the heavy responsibilities of that field. Just like moon there is a brighter side and a darker side having a lot of crates, cliffs and falls which can be crossed only by an expert in the principles of human psychology because a CEO is essentially a leader of a talent pool.

How to identifying seeds from weeds is our basic concern of a researcher in developing a CEO. Excellence in Management occurs when the role giving matches with role taking while this process remains very complex due to the fact the role taker is one but the role givers are many. That , accordingly leads us to the point that the Head of an Organization has to have a personality *of unitas multiplex* covering right emotions, right skills and right knowledge.

An Excellent HR Manager is a basically an healthy person with essential professional virtues. He loves his job, continuously develops his skills, takes initiative in spite of all unfavorable circumstances and feels capable to perform his duties in all situations. He carries on his duties hopefully and completes responsibilities with total trust on people. He accepts his role willingly. He never reduces his willingness and energy in fulfilling his role, his main focus being their growth and development of employees. A boss has to avoid all types of prejudices ranging from attitudes, opinions ,race, gender, color , religion, region,

HRD FOR CEO

The level of development can be assessed with an instrument to measure the skills and abilities and behavioral sensitivity of a CEO .At the lowest rung lies his technical skills and at the highest level is his skills to handle HRD techniques for workers.

The issues that have remained unattended so far are freedom ,dignity and self-worth of workers, developing autonomous work group, quality of work life of workers , development of skills required for growth of workers .In this case some common techniques are job rotation, Job redesign with job enrichment, job enlargement, democracy at work.

People generally compare the value of their own with those of others in similar work situations based on their inputs and outputs. Everybody wants to be treated equally and fairly. Pains in the heart are deeper due to perceived unfairness at work. This feeling - real or imaginary- requires to be removed early.

MANAGEMENT BIASES

From the beginning of his career a CEO might have come across many coworkers who have had helped him, supported him and even encouraged him. It is rational; one should not forget them. During crises, bad times and good times, ups and downs, during happy time and distressful time only our near by workers come to our rescue. Taking charge of his own development a CEO assigns maximum value to establishing relationship with workers as they are the asset builders of the company .It means providing support, encouragement and a guiding them in the developmental path is a human approach. There are many workers who look to the boss as his god and savior. One can't overlook their feelings and performances. A CEO has to maintain a record of all the contributions that a worker makes and converts them into monitory form and then examines how the worker needs his support during his difficulties, work challenges and conflicts faced by him at work. All CEO performances are the product of sincere efforts of dedicated workers. How can their contribution be overlooked in order to gain a little personal benefit. He has to avoid showing extra attention to people who take additional pains to gain the favor of bosses. He has to avoid who have negative intentions attitudes and behavior. Not recognizing good performance is definitely demoralizing .In order to avoid extra efforts bosses make clustering or group the into average performers. This is harmful to the organization> It is dangerous to try to take revenge for a head of the organization. The Head of an organization has a special responsibility of avoiding any prejudices ranging from attitudes, opinions ,race, gender ,age , religion to skin color. A persons contribution is the sum total of his efforts, energy and skills applied at work. One has to avoid decisions on the basis of recent events since a worker has shown loyalty for a long time before.

There need to be separate systems for development and for rewards. More rigorous application analysis techniques and recording events are required to link assessment of a mangers with rewards. Similar are the steps the managers have to follow while assessing a worker.

ASSESSMENT OF QWL

A CEO, who doesn't care for the quality of life of a small worker can't find QWL in his own case. If he has worked hard to gain his position he would have found joy in his work because joy is the expression of satisfaction in work of an achieving man. This also comes from a man who has a feeling of thankfulness towards all those workers who has silently toiled to see that the company achieves it goal under the stewardship of the CEO. Serenity ,not, anxiety is the sign of good performance. One who knows the goal and the path can't find journey confusing. An achieving executive is always curious for innovative and creative ways and means. A hard working man is always hopeful. A CEO gets inspiration from the efforts and success of his workers. In an organization the highest motivated person is no other person than the CEO. His motivation also comes from his attachment to his workers. They are his true means of his cheerfulness. He carries a positive feeling that things will mostly workout in his organization. That feeling wave is passed on throughout the industry. A man who believes in himself can only create this feeling in others. Love and happiness go together. A CEO gets happiness by putting the needs of workers ahead of his own.

CORRUPTION DUE TO POWER

Most organizations today suffer from anger, fear, sadness, loneliness, melancholy and annoyance. These all happen right under the nose of a CEO. When nobody is happy, there can't be QWL for a CEO. Since a CEO has been bestowed with unlimited power in the organization that could be the cause of his most unhappiness. He asks more for himself. He spend more for his own happiness. He never gets this. He becomes arrogant and more self-centered. He tends to use more power for himself and his limited family. He even his trusted workers as instruments for his personal gains. Day after day he remains immersed in abysmal anxieties.

Trust, affection and closeness with workers may have check on his tendency for corruption. Differences with anybody in the hierarchy may be treated as feedback and analyzed threadbare for the subject matter, means ,methods and agents of communication. Differences should not emotions and emotional outbursts. His reaction should not be on the person, his personality or his behavior. On the contrary the communication should continue on intention, goal and performance.

When an employee throws his opinion before the higher authority he expresses his feedback along with emotional difficulties on the order, system, procedure or instruction. The listener needs to understand the difficulty and try to remove the constraints.

In maintaining worker relationship the CEO accepts the workers as they are, giving rise to new process of mutual acceptance of strengths and weaknesses. With this recognition and acknowledgement of their difficulties workers gradually start trusting and listening .Then problem solving becomes easy.

When the management says they own the workers it is not so easy in practice. They need to change their attitudes .They have to make an effort to reach every person under them with direct communication, notes , circular or letter. Some good managers follow social rituals like calling the person on phone on social occasions or otherwise .Relationship can also be maintained through outside activities like sports and culture, education and religious functions. Opportunities at the time of retirement or illness can be utilized for exchanging their goodwill. All these activities finally establish a strong emotional bond between the workers and the management.

CORE VALUES OF HUMAN RELATIONSHIP

An excellent CEO has time for even the lowest rung of the employees. Most probably he structures his time in such a manner that it does not affect his urgent work. He trusts his employees and does not hesitate to share all information that affect employees .He is willing to share resources in work and outside work with his employees. He is committed to their growth and development. Since he is primarily loyal to the organization there can't be any conflict with his commitment to his workers. He puts the needs of others before his own. He shows gratitude by appreciating both quality and quantity of work of others.

He never monopolizes credit. He shows hope even in adverse circumstances .For him a worker is a real brother. He does not lead a flamboyant life style and remains a model for others. He is inspirational and comfortable with self. He is self-disciplined. He has patience .He doesn't manipulate his subordinates for his personal gain. He does not show his rage , particularly in public since failures are considered as opportunities for improvement. He avoids impulsiveness. He is neither suspicious nor jealous.

ANGER MANAGEMENT

Anger management is as important as fulfilling one's responsibilities. One of the primary causes of anger is facing hurdles while one is using all energies in order to reach his goal. Anger also arises out of stress of work and illness due to unhealthy work environment .The earliest hurdle in the path of a CEO is resources constraint .He leverages integrators as well as team members. When required he does not hesitate to use advanced technology in place of human beings to reduce their boredom or monotony..

COMPETITION

Nobody can avoid competition in a global business environment .What he can do is to strengthen his strengths and weaken his weaknesses .In order to face time constraints he prioritizes tasks as per their urgency and importance.

ORGANIZATIONAL POLITICS

Politics is essentially a power game. A large organization is power house of resources. That raises the political sentiments of people who has a large resources . They are eager to play politics and become centers of power. A CEO always remains above organizational politics. He avoids taking action impulsively or in rage. He obtains all necessary information before taking a decision .He always takes decisions constructively and in favor of the organization . He is not part of any power center.

ECONOMIC SITUATION

For meeting a future crises or downtime a developed CEO continuously arranges for risk audit. A fool proof plan for facing unknown challenges includes developing a disaster management team. He studies the past history and tries to predict the disasters in advance keeping an alternative plan ready. A future ready CEO is up-to-date with trends and uncertainty.

When QWL is the focus of every manager they will create a culture of management by relationship. When relationships improve trust ,listening, acceptance and communication becomes the order . In this culture every one will be an Achiever.

"Life doesn't make any sense without interdependence. We need each other, and the sooner we learn that, the better for us all." –Erik Erikson

"Once you start making the effort to 'wake yourself up'—that is, be more mindful in your activities—you suddenly start appreciating life a lot more." –Robert Biswas-Diener

"We are what we are because we have been what we have been, and what is needed for solving the problems of human life and motives is not moral estimates but more knowledge." –Sigmund Freud

CHAPTER 6

LEARNING WHILE DOING

MENTORING

The mentor and mentee relationship starts when the mentee approaches a specific mentor after he studies the background of the chosen mentor. It is followed by a few sessions of dialogue and explorations about each other. Then they study personal profiles, common interests and possibilities. It is followed by mutual acceptance of the relationship. Documentation may also be done.

A learner from a learned and experienced senior on whom he has trust seeks the mentoring support . He believes that his relationship with the mentor will provide ample opportunities for developing his skills. He knows that the mentor will neither exploit his weakness nor misuse any information that he shares with him. The mentor is capable of understanding the needs and expectations of the under-study. The relationship has to be guided by mutual respect.

The mentor plays the role of an expert as well as a role model. By -and- by the mentor helps the mentee understand the organizational behavior, the social equations, office politics and explore new and conflicting ideas. He helps the mentee to remove his weaknesses. In the process the mentor checks the progress of the mentee and puts him on the right track. He shares his personal experiences. The mentee listens to ideas, learns the skills and becomes self-aware. The mentee remains cautious not to seek solutions or answers to constraints directly. He takes responsibilities and learns the methods of analysis. He develops confidence by self-help.

COACHING

Coaching is an effective method to develop a present and a future manager. It is a process to raise the manager's awareness of his style and behavior. In this process the superior or an experienced Manager takes the responsibility of developing his subordinate's skills.

The Coach takes initiative to create a psychologically safe environment for learning. He supports, and doesn't condemn. A successful coaching program has focus on coachee's goal, priorities and agenda. The coaching process has to be conversational. The facilitator gives options and suggestions, not direct answers. While coaching an adult the principle of learning by experience plays an important role. They discuss past and analyze what went well and didn't. For strengthening the relationship the coach shows his belief on the potential of the coachee. He always tries to bring the best in him. While remaining flexible he gives him challenges in a progressive manner. His teaching methods are participative. He often uses questioning method for developing his abilities to reflect.

OBSERVING

The CEO observes a certain model persons to improve his

role effectiveness. Role modeling is a powerful technique of learning for an executive. He learns from his model not only consciously but also unconsciously. He studies their knowledge, skills and values and tries to practice them. He analyses their behavior and makes a comparison to find where he needs to catch up. He also discusses with his role model in order to reflect upon the positive elements.

EXPERIMENTS

Some advanced executives experiment new management

models to better understand events and situations. from time . They refine and adjust their models on the basis of their results. This becomes a co

REFLECTING

To see and understand the "big picture." one reflects on various case studies. He reads, stops and thinks.as to how he can use them in his work. He also arranges discussions on interesting topics for general discussion.

SELF-INTEGRATION AND INSIGHT DEVELOPMENT

Periodically the CEO arranges for meeting of self-learning

groups. In this group executives compile, analyze and integrate all the data and develop understanding on problems and solutions. They analyze each other's mind, body and emotions. They use mindfulness and meditation to see within themselves. They also experiment their own behavior in this laboratory like situation.

CHAPTER 7

THE BUCK STOPS HERE

For centuries together man has remained in search of an all- powerful entity to solve his problems and improve the quality of life. It invented new technologies to build power but it failed to enrich man's life.

He now has pinned his hope on modern business and its CEO

to give him solace, we-feeling, peace, safety and security and return his freedom, dignity and self worth.

It is not fair to use a perfect scale to measure the imperfect surface of the moon. Many unskilled and semi-skilled workers run most of the routine tasks in metropolis. A worker who comes in search of his daily bread is born and brought up in an unhealthy remote village. We can't expect him to be very cultured and civil in his daily routine. He had his little education in a little village school. How can we put him to test on a sophisticated scale and ask him to compete with an urban grown and public school educated young man? This seems to be social injustice. This type of injustice is clear in case of migrant workers and slum dwellers in cities. They run our business to the extent of fifty percent.

Most developed countries and civilizations take pride in

treating their women workers as subservient to male workers. They are not paid same wages for same work. They are not given equal promotional opportunities. In business decisions their ideas are not given equal value. Before the CEO takes up his new assignment it is essential that he is given sensitivity training in order to develop empathy towards such groups and such issues so that future conflicts can be avoided.

The development requirements are same for both rich and poor . Similarly their requirements are same even if their society standards are different. But industry being a rational organization it can't continue with irrational treatments. It will still be better when learned and prosperous people try to correct the past mistakes by taking additional steps.

In this type of an unequal competition the CEO has a primary responsibility to protect his workers and give them ample initial opportunities to develop and grow in the organization with others.

The achieving CEO develops a long term but rolling business strategy, He contributes in strengthening an open social system that can promote his business. He makes his human resources enabling and competent. He develops systems and procedures that facilitate decision implementation easy. He makes managers people oriented.

He builds team of performing executives who are ever prepared to work as the CEO.

CHAPTER 8

THINKS AND ACTS LIKE A CEO

A dead man cannot lift even a pin. But an energetic man can destroy Hiroshima and Nagasaki in no time. There is power in thinking. That thinking comes from change of vision. An achiever has an achieving vision for him as well as for all who come in contact with him.

By habit ,all of us think small. We limit our thoughts to the tasks assigned to us. If not assigned, we may stick to what is written in books. The CEO needs to overcome that habit. He needs to think in terms of more achievements , better work-life and more happiness for himself and for others.

The tasks he undertakes needs to end with success.

For that he needs to plan in advance, acquire resources, be clear about the methods and tools and then undertakes confident action. He needs to think of solutions in constraints , not problems. Some may feed him with a lot of negative data. His mind may get fixed with excuses like age , health etc. He just needs to change that thinking and start with bold steps.

Sometimes the forces of fear of many kinds may paralyze him. Only small steps of positive action can destroy fear.

A CEO has to have a large vision. He needs to think in creative way. He makes it a habit to get associated with people and places, which have success- experiences. Here his preconceived attitudes matter a lot. He gives a touch of class to everything he does and every word he speaks.

CORE VALUES OF MEANINGFUL RELATIONSHIP AT WORK :

INITIATIVE

He initiates measures to decentralize decisions and introduces a flat structure. He introduces all such measures that help in improving workers' commitment to organization.

TRUST

He is trust worthy. His deeds synchronize with his words. He never fails to keep his promises to workers or their unions. His principles are consistent for all cadres of employees. He trusts his employees and does not hesitate to share all information that affect employees .He is willing to share resources , in -work and outside -work , with his employees. He is committed to their satisfaction as well as their growth and development.

TIME

He spares time for the needs satisfaction of the workers. He studies theirs interests ,education and experience and helps assign job that match these worker abilities and skills, keeping their satisfaction in view.

INSPIRATION

By being enthusiastic and energetic he inspires his team members. He energizes them by improving their quality of work life.

SHARING RESOURCES

He shares powers with lower cadres and collaborates with them in thick and thin.

COMMITMENT

He has positive feelings for his job, organization and business. He has sense of obligation towards them. He is accountable for his action and of others. He appreciates and improves others at work.

LOYALTY

He is loyal to the organization that has recognized his talent and put him at the helm of the affairs.

RELATIONS ORIENTED

With People first style of management he builds a long term productive relationship.

HUMILITY

He does not hanker after personal rewards and benefits. On the contrary he inspires loyalty of others. He showers all credit to workers.

HOPE

Things and events have only limited effects on results .They can always be changed by people with extra efforts and greater energy. All bad times will end in good times. The CEO creates this feeling among workers.

BROTHERHOOD

Take active interest in the desires, and goals of workers and juniors. He respects other people's beliefs and opinions. He teaches through examples. He treats them as equal partners and co-travelers.

JUSTICE-FAIR TREATMENT

He never allows anybody to develop a feeling of injustice as he never fails to give fair opportunities and benefits to all.

SOCIAL PROGRESS

The CEO tries more for the social and community progress of workers rather than individual progress.

FAMILY FEELING

An excellent CEO has time for even the lowest rung of the employees. Most probably he structures his time in such a manner that it does not affect his urgent work.

He creates the workplace as an association of family members with the help of brotherhood feeling. He joins workers at work as well as in their leisure activities. He cares for their families also.

COMMUNICATION

He enjoys explaining details of complex jobs, technology or projects being introduced.

POSITIVE EMOTIONS

The CEO helps the employees to do their best and feel the joy of their achievements. He never losses opportunity to thank them individually as well as in groups so that they also learn the importance of gratitude and humility. The CEO never expresses dissatisfaction on anything relating to his present or past. About his family or relatives including the coworkers. This should reflect in his being calm and peaceful feeling due to self-acceptance. He is lively . He shows interests and curiosity about things and people around him. All these good emotions are actually meant to be imbibed by his workers as he is their first teacher. He is eager and optimistic.

Besides making a worker feel good , positive emotions of a superior have an important place in his productivity. Positive emotions create an environment of joy that can't be created by any material gift. Your sharing the same dining table over a working lunch , the joy of handling an innovative product launched in the market for first time and greatly accepted by the consumers or receiving a first time certificate of merit are all memorable for the whole life. They are great career builders too.

The social environment where the growth-oriented Executive leads the company as a CEO healthy interpersonal and inter-group relationships form the foundation of their existence. Each individual and each group works as a supporter, an encouraging and understanding partner for each other. Warmth and mutual respect is their actual source of satisfaction and stability.

GRATITUDE

Gratitude is a common positive emotion that can strengthen manger's relationship with workers. He can simply say" thank you " when a work is completed or keeps a workplace neat and clean or just they listen to you. It builds trust and closeness.

FORGIVE

At work, with eagerness to do our best it is normal for disagreements to arise among staff. The CEO as the head has to show a model behavior by forgetting and forgiving the differences. It helps them to think for tomorrow.

COMPASSION

It is impossible to realize the feelings that one get due to loss of money, prestige or status at work. The CEO recognizes and acknowledges others pains when they comes to his notice and empathizes by being present when needed.

ACCEPT OTHERS

As workers some of the employees may have weaknesses. They have strengths too. Accept them as they are as natural beings. You may give your support to change their skills for better performance when mutually agreed upon.

SOCIAL TIME

Worker-manager relationship can be meaningful and productive when it is enriched with social activities together. They may create some rituals like meeting at private functions, exchanging good wishes over phone or by writing letters. That may not lead you to be with them all the time. They need to have some private time also.

He puts the needs of others before his own. He shows gratitude by appreciating both quality and quantity of work of others. He never monopolizes credit. He shows hope even in adverse circumstances .For him a worker is a real brother. He does not lead a flamboyant life style. He is a model for others. He is inspirational and comfortable with self. He is self-disciplined. He has patience .He doesn't manipulate his subordinates for his personal gain.

ANGER MANAGEMENT

He does not show his rage in public since failures are considered as opportunities for improvement. He avoids impulsiveness. He is neither suspicious nor jealous.

Anger management is as important as fulfilling one's responsibilities. One of the primary causes of anger is facing hurdles while one is using all energies in order to reach his goal. The earliest hurdle in the path of a CEO is resources constraint .He leverages integrators as well as team members. When required he does not hesitate to use advanced technology in place of human being.

COMPETITION

Nobody can avoid competition in a global business. What he can do is to strengthen his strengths and weaken his weaknesses .In order to face time constraints he prioritizes tasks as per their urgency and importance.

ORGANIZATIONAL POLITICS

He always remains above organizational politics. He

avoids taking action in rage or impulsively. He obtains all necessary information before taking a decision. He always takes decisions constructively and in favor of the organization.

ECONOMIC SITUATION

For meeting a future crises or downtime a developed CEO continuously arranges for risk audit. A fool proof plan for facing unknown challenges includes developing a disaster management team. He studies the past history and tries to predict the disasters in advance keeping an alternative plan ready. A future - ready CEO is up-to-date with trends and uncertainties.

CHAPTER 9

THE INTEGRATION

The CEO has the ultimate goal of integrating people with organization and the organization with the people. He integrates the machine culture with human culture, and the Manager's culture with worker's culture.

Workers have talents of sincerity ,hard work ,commitment , loyalty ,dedication and service orientation. On the other hand, the managers are generally more educated. They have greater ability to learn, knowledge , resourcefulness ,emotional maturity and creativity.

The CEO tries to integrate these talents both can become one .Both the groups identify themselves into one achieving team called the corporation. In doing so all of them experience growth and fulfillment.

Fueling, oiling, maintaining and replacing characterize machine culture. People are treated as nothing more than machine parts. Here responsibilities are assigned and rewarded as per results. As against this a team is considered as a cooperative and supportive group. They are friendly and nurturing. Responsibilities are volunteered and the group gets recognition and from it the individuals.

His field of work is beyond his cabin. He walks all around the places that his people are found to be busy at work. Sometimes he sees more than what is visible before his eyes. He also sees the dedication and toil of people in his mind's eye. He collects data not only what is available on paper. He periodically interacts with people and tries to get meaning from the silence of workers who provide uninterrupted essential services like power, water, transport, security and related facilities. He takes special care to listen to the innumerable silent male and female workers who give their attendance before the factory time in order to keep the premises neat and clean, and hygienic. They are the silent warriors who defy all hazards of nature. He represents the voice and the face of his people.

www.ingramcontent.com/pod-product-compliance
Lightning Source LLC
Chambersburg PA
CBHW031625210526
45464CB00004B/1756